7-14

D1514740

TRAILBLAZING THE WAY WEST

ARCTURUS

ARCTURUS

This edition first published in 2015 by Arcturus Publishing

Distributed by Black Rabbit Books
P.O. Box 3263
Mankato
Minnesota MN 56002

Text: Frederick Nolan
Design: Chris Bell
Cover design: Akihiro Nakayama
Original concept design: Keith Williams
Project editors: JMS books
Project manager: Joe Harris

Copyright © Arcturus Holdings Limited

Cataloging-in-Publication Data is available from the Library of Congress

ISBN: 978-1-78404-081-9

Printed in China

SL003861US
Supplier 29, Date 0514, Print Run 3424

THE WILD WEST

TRAILBLAZING THE WAY WEST

"Go West, young man, and grow up
with the country."

Horace Greeley (1811–72), U.S. politician and journalist.

CONTENTS

Introduction 6

⸻⸻

The Lewis and Clark Expedition 7

⸻⸻

Mountain Men 15

⸻⸻

The Great Pathfinders 25

⸻⸻

Pushing Westward 33

⸻⸻

The Battle of the Alamo 41

⸻⸻

The Donner Party 51

⸻⸻

Glossary 61

⸻⸻

Further Information 62

⸻⸻

Index 63

⸻⸻

INTRODUCTION

FOR THOSE AMERICANS of European ancestry living in the eastern part of the United States at the turn of the 19th century, the "far western frontier" was the Mississippi River. So, in 1803 when Thomas Jefferson purchased the 820,000 square miles (2,123,800 sq km) of French-owned land called Louisiana, thereby increasing the national territory by 140 per cent, the area to the west, beyond the river, was the great unknown. The first of the settlers to venture past this and the Missouri River and head into uncharted territory were the mountain men and pathfinders, and adventurers like Lewis and Clark. But what began as isolated exploratory expeditions would eventually become a constant flow as more and more settlers headed west.

However, for the Native Americans—the many different tribes and ethnic groups who populated the American continent—the push westward was a bitter experience. A large number of them were nomadic cultures, moving from place to place with the seasons, living as hunter-gatherers. As the settlers traveled across their lands and the tribes found themselves displaced and ultimately dispossessed of their ancestral lands, some felt bound to resist and conflict was inevitable.

Still, the migration of the settlers proved unstoppable, and by the end of century the population had increased to over seventy-five million and the prairies and mountains were dotted with new cities and towns, like Chicago, Milwaukee, Kansas City, Denver.... Railroads linked east and west and the "frontier" no longer existed—the United States had metamorphosed into a mighty nation stretching "from sea to shining sea."

Westward Ho! *(Emanuel Leutze, 1816–68).*

THE LEWIS AND CLARK EXPEDITION

Meriwether Lewis and William Clark at the mouth of the Columbia River during their exploration of the Louisiana Territory (Frederic Remington, 1861–1909).

INTO THE UNKNOWN

ON APRIL 30, 1803, PRESIDENT

THOMAS JEFFERSON—WHO HAD BEGUN NEGOTIATIONS SEEKING ONLY TO BUY THE PORT OF NEW ORLEANS—DOUBLED THE SIZE OF THE INFANT UNITED STATES FOR A MERE $15 MILLION BY CONCLUDING with Emperor Napoleon the purchase of some 820,000 sq miles (2,123,800 sq km) of mostly unexplored French-owned land in central North America, bounded to the west by Spanish California and known as Louisiana. The first priority, the president decided, was to find out exactly what lay out there beyond the "frontier" and he persuaded Congress to finance a voyage of exploration that would establish whether there was a route across this vast and unknown country to the Pacific.

AT THIS TIME the Missouri River had been charted only as far as the villages of the Mandan Native Americans in the Dakota region. What lay between there and the Pacific coast, or how far one was from the other, none of the east coast settlers knew. Some believed there were mountains made entirely of salt; others that California was an island. Stories abounded of strange tribes living in the wilderness: warrior-like, man-hating Amazon women; a tribe of Welsh-speaking Native Americans descended from a man who had reached America

Mandan Native Americans.

Commander Captain Meriwether Lewis (top) and Second Lieutenant William Clark (bottom).

before Columbus; and a community of small, knee-high devils in human form. Some settlers believed that Native Americans might be descendants of the lost tribes of Israel.

The man Jefferson chose to establish what was legend and what was fact was his thirty-year-old personal secretary, soldier, and scholar Captain Meriwether Lewis. He in turn selected as his coleader William Clark, a younger brother of the famous soldier and frontiersman George Rogers Clark, who had conquered the country west of the Allegheny Mountains during the American Revolution. They were to prove a good team: throughout the expedition Lewis's better education and scientific training were perfectly complemented by Clark's practical ability and understanding of frontier survival, and there was never a single incidence of tension or rivalry between them.

They left Wood River, near the mouth of the Missouri River, on May 14, 1804, in two *pirogues* (long, narrow canoes made from a single tree trunk) and a keelboat 60 ft (18.3 m) long— a large, flat freight barge, pulled by horses or by hand. They traveled up the Missouri, reaching the villages of the Mandan Native Americans at the mouth of the Knife River in what is now North Dakota on October 26, where they spent the winter and where the only man to perish on the journey, Clark's servant Charles Floyd, died of peritonitis—inflammation of the lining of the abdomen.

THE CORPS OF DISCOVERY

THE EXPEDITION RESUMED ITS

JOURNEY IN THE APRIL OF 1805, THE PARTY NOW REDUCED TO THIRTY-THREE MEN—AND ONE WOMAN. THIS WAS THE HEAVILY pregnant Shoshone translator and guide named Sacajawea.

THE CORPS OF Discovery—the "official" name of the expedition—made every effort to meet peacefully with the more than fifty tribes of Native Americans they encountered, to try to understand their customs and to cement cordial relations between them and the "Great White Father," as they described the president. They presented the Native American leaders with presents—colored beads, calico shirts, mirrors, bells, needles, ribbons, kettles, and rings—and where appropriate, special "peace tokens" struck by Jefferson for just this purpose. They

Lewis and Clark hold council with the Native Americans.

would prove so successful in this mission that a number of Native American delegations went east to meet Jefferson even before Lewis and Clark had returned.

The expedition reached the Great Falls of the Missouri in present-day Montana in June, crossed the Stony (Rocky) Mountains, and descended the Columbia River to the Oregon Territory and the Pacific Ocean, which they reached November 7, 1805. With no friendly Native Americans to shelter them this time, and unable to find any ships to take them back east, they constructed Fort Clatsop where they endured a particularly dreadful winter.

They started their return journey on March 23, 1806, then split up, with Clark leading an exploration of the Yellowstone guided by Sacajawea, while Lewis led a party of nine men over the Rockies via what is now called Lewis and Clark Pass and reached the upper Missouri on July 11. While awaiting the arrival of Clark, Lewis took three men to explore the Marias River. It was here that the only serious clash with Native Americans took place. Feeling threatened by the terms of a peace agreement, under

SACAJAWEA

Sacajawea (meaning "Bird Woman") was a Shoshone woman married to a member of the expedition, Toussaint Charbonneau. Although she was pregnant, Lewis decided to take her along with him and she became an invaluable asset to the expedition, acting as their interpreter and intermediary with the various Native American tribes they encountered. Lewis, who called her "Jenny" and Clark, who called her "Janey" both spoke very highly of her talents, and Clark, in particular, was much taken by Sacajawea's infant son, Jean Baptiste, to whom he gave the nickname "Pompey," meaning headman.

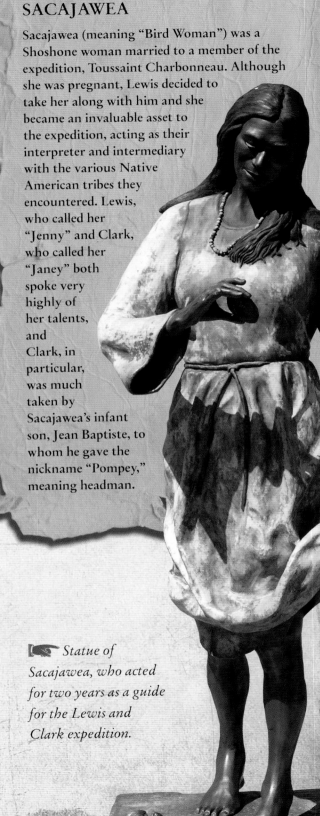

☞ *Statue of Sacajawea, who acted for two years as a guide for the Lewis and Clark expedition.*

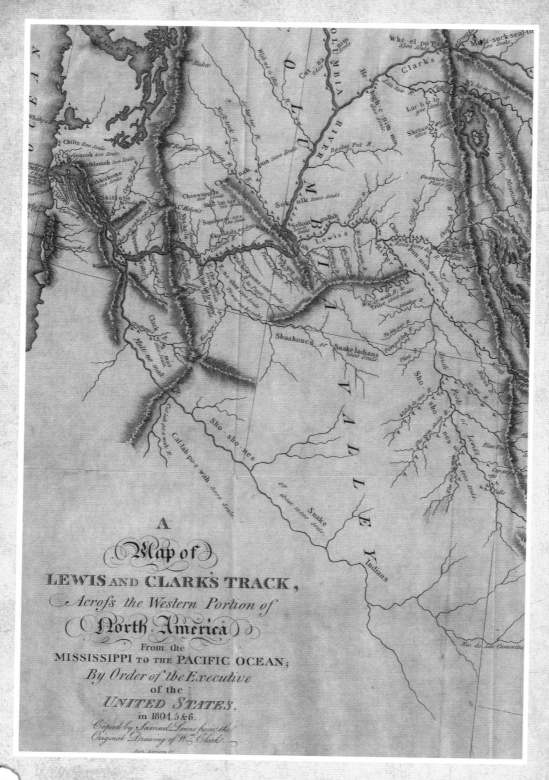

A
Map of
LEWIS AND CLARK'S TRACK,
Across the Western Portion of
North America
From the
MISSISSIPPI TO THE PACIFIC OCEAN;
By Order of the Executive
of the
UNITED STATES,
in 1804. 5 & 6.
Copied by Samuel Lewis from the
Original Drawing of W.ᵐ Clark.

Lewis and Clark's expedition changed the mapping of northwest America by providing the first accurate depiction of the sources of the Columbia and Missouri Rivers and the Rocky Mountains. This 1814 map was based on William Clark's manuscript map.

which the United States intended to give guns to the Shoshone and Nez Perce (enemies of the Blackfeet), two Blackfeet were killed as they tried to steal horses and weapons from Lewis's camp, one by Lewis himself. Lewis then hurried to his rendezvous with Clark, fearful that more Blackfeet might come after them. None did, although a result of this encounter was that the Blackfeet remained hostile toward the settlers for years. Just a few days later, on August 12, Clark rejoined Lewis near the mouth of the Yellowstone only to find that the preceding day Lewis had been shot through the thigh by Pierre Cruzatte, a member of the party and former fur trader, who had mistaken him for an elk.

Lewis's wound healed within a month, by which time they were pushing back down the Missouri, reaching St. Louis on September 23, 1806, after an absence of two years, four months, and nine days. They had covered 7,689 miles (12,302 km), and brought back countless specimens of plants and wildlife, as well as journals bulging with geographic and topographical information. The Lewis and Clark expedition, originally budgeted at $2,500 (though the final cost was $38,722.25) remains probably the most significant feat of exploration in the history of the United States until the moon landing.

The expedition trail ran from the plains of the Midwest to the shores of the Pacific Ocean and back again.

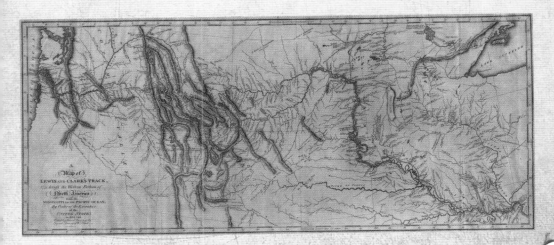

THE AFTERMATH

TO REWARD THEIR SUCCESS,

THOMAS JEFFERSON APPOINTED LEWIS GOVERNOR OF LOUISIANA TERRITORY, THE COUNTRY THROUGH WHICH HE HAD TRAVELED, WHILE CLARK, WHO RESIGNED FROM THE ARMY IN FEBRUARY 1807, WAS MADE Louisiana's Brigadier General of Militia and principal Indian agent— an intermediary between the U.S. government and the tribes.

MERIWETHER LEWIS died in mysterious circumstances—possibly suicide, maybe murder—in 1809. In 1813 Clark was named governor of the Missouri Territory and lived long enough to serve under five presidents; awarded many honors, he died at St. Louis on September 1, 1838. He persuaded Sacajawea, who had remained at the Mandan villages with her husband Charbonneau, to come to St. Louis and, according to one story, they left their son Jean Baptiste with Clark to be educated. Later, a daughter, Lizette, also reached St. Louis and Clark became her guardian, too. Many historians believe Sacajawea died in 1812, while others contend that she lived among her people in Wyoming until she was about one hundred years old and died on April 9, 1884. Whichever is true, there are many monuments to her at places related to her life.

William Clark's tomb, Bellefontaine Cemetery, St. Louis.

MOUNTAIN MEN

Trappers *(Alfred Jacob Miller, 1810–74).*

KINGS OF THE WILD FRONTIER

IN THE FOOTSTEPS OF LEWIS

AND CLARK CAME A HARDY BREED OF EXPLORERS AND FRONTIERSMEN WHO VENTURED FEARLESSLY INTO THE UNEXPLORED WILDERNESS, BLAZING TRAILS THAT WITHIN A FEW SHORT DECADES WOULD BE utilized by first a trickle, then a flood of pioneering emigrants heading west in search of new lands, new lives, and adventure.

MEANWHILE, A NEW industry was blossoming—the fur trade. Europeans had been buying American furs since the 16th century, when the French had controlled and capitalized on the trade. After the French came the English and the Dutch, and then at the beginning of the 19th century a new breed of entrepreneurs, men like John Jacob Astor, Manuel Lisa, and Pierre Chouteau, who set out to challenge the former dominance of British and French organizations like the Hudson's Bay Company and the North West Company.

John Jacob Astor amassed a huge fortune and became a leading figure in the fur trade.

It was with this 1822 call to young, adventurous men that the fur trade got fully into its stride. This advertisement was to have far-reaching effects upon the history of the American West:

TO ENTERPRISING YOUNG MEN

THE SUBSCRIBER WISHES TO ENGAGE ONE HUNDRED MEN, TO ASCEND THE RIVER MISSOURI TO ITS SOURCE, THERE TO BE EMPLOYED FOR ONE, TWO, OR THREE YEARS. FOR PARTICULARS ENQUIRE OF MAJOR ANDREW HENRY, NEAR THE LEAD MINES, IN THE COUNTY OF WASHINGTON (WHO WILL ASCEND WITH, AND COMMAND THE PARTY) OR TO THE SUBSCRIBER AT ST. LOUIS.

Wm. H. Ashley

The first boatload of William Ashley's trappers—among them an eighteen-year-old apprentice named Jim Bridger, twenty-three-year-old Jedediah Smith, riverboat man Mike Fink, Thomas Fitzpatrick, William Sublette, and Hugh Glass—headed up the Missouri River toward "the shining mountains." In the wilderness these "company men" and others, rugged individualists all, would hunt, trap, and skin countless beaver and other fur-bearing animals, then bring their bounty out of the mountains to a prearranged meeting with the fur traders. In the summer of 1825, over one hundred of them appeared in the foothills of the Uinta Mountains of Utah to trade their catches for money, supplies—and whiskey—the first "rendezvous," as these annual gatherings became known. For the next three decades the fur trade would rule the West.

Jedediah Smith's party crossing the burning Mojave Desert during the 1826 trek to California (by Frederic Remington, 1799–1831).

BRIDGER, KING OF THE MOUNTAIN MEN

APPRENTICED TO A ST. LOUIS

BLACKSMITH AT THE AGE OF FOURTEEN, JIM BRIDGER LEFT FOR THE MOUNTAINS FOUR YEARS LATER AND IT WOULD BE ANOTHER SEVENTEEN YEARS BEFORE HE CAME BACK. HE WAS IN THE PARTY that abandoned Hugh Glass in 1823; the following year he discovered the Great Salt Lake, which he at first believed was the Pacific Ocean. Bridger's descriptions of his discoveries—such as the geysers in what is now Yellowstone Park—were often at first disbelieved ("They said I was the damnedest liar ever lived," he complained); as a result he took pleasure in telling "tall stories" about his exploits to gullible listeners.

IN 1830 BRIDGER became one of the organizers of the Rocky Mountain Fur Company, trapping in Blackfoot country and participating in the battle with Blackfoot warriors at Pierre's Hole on July 18, 1832. Although he was illiterate, Bridger was a shrewd judge of character. When the Rocky Mountain Fur Company was dissolved in 1834, he teamed up with Tom Fitzpatrick and Milton Sublette.

Jim Bridger's strong constitution allowed him to survive extreme conditions while exploring the Rocky Mountains.

Castle Geyser, Yellowstone National Park.

The following winter he was back in Blackfoot country with Joe Meek and Kit Carson, and married a Flathead Native American woman, with whom he had several children.

In 1838 Bridger joined the American Fur Company and with Louis Vasquez began construction of Fort Bridger in Wyoming. It became one of the principal trading posts on the Oregon Trail, a military post, and a Pony Express station. After his first wife died, Bridger married two more Native American women in succession. He hired a boy to read Shakespeare aloud to him and often quoted the Bard.

Ousted from Fort Bridger by the Mormons in 1853, he guided General Albert Sidney Johnston's column to Salt Lake City during the so-called Mormon War of 1857–58. After guiding Captain William F. Raynolds's Yellowstone Expedition (1859–60), Captain Edward L. Berthoud's engineering party (1861), and the ill-fated Powder River Expedition (1865–66), Bridger settled near Westport, Missouri, where he later bought a farm. His health began to fail, and in 1873 he went blind. He died on July 17, 1878, just three days after Sheriff Pat Garrett killed Billy the Kid at Fort Sumner. A down-to-earth frontiersman, he was one of the most able, best liked, and famous of all the mountain men.

JOHN COLTER, LEGEND OF THE WEST

THE EARLY MOUNTAIN MEN,

OR "VOYAGEURS," AS THEY SOMETIMES CALLED THEMSELVES, WERE FIRST DRAWN TO THE VIRGIN FORESTS AND RIVERS OF THE WEST AS TRAPPERS AND TRADERS. INITIALLY THERE WERE JUST A FEW trapping beaver, otter, mink, and marten in what are now Colorado and Wyoming. Men like "Old Bill" Williams, Jim Beckwourth, and the legendary "Liver Eating" Johnson went each year into the wilderness to find new rivers and fresh hunting grounds. Many of them never came back: only the toughest survived. The story of one of them, John Colter, illustrates graphically just how tough it was.

COLTER WAS A loner. He was out in the wilderness trapping furs long before Lewis and Clark's expedition found its way to the mountains. In his search for furs, Colter was the first man to see what is now Yellowstone Park, but no one would believe his stories of steaming hot springs and geysers spouting a hundred feet into the air. In 1808 he and another trapper, John Potts, strayed too far into Blackfoot territory and were surrounded by some five hundred Native Americans. Angered by Colter's previous mission to the Crow, the Blackfeet felt that both the settlers and the Crow were encroaching on their lands.

☞ "Old Bill" Williams (Alfred Jacob Miller, 1810–74).

Blackfoot warriors.

Ten days and 250 miles (400 km) later, starving and dehydrated, his feet torn, his skin blistered from the sun and full of festering thorns, he reached Fort Lisa at the mouth of the Bighorn River. Amazingly, after a short recuperation, Colter went back to the mountains trapping for fur. It's said that in 1810, after another encounter with the Native Americans, in which several of his friends were killed, Colter swore to quit trapping and "be damned if I ever come into it again." Using his profits from the fur trade, he returned to St. Louis, where he became a neighbor of frontiersman Daniel Boone, got married, and had a son. He died in 1813, aged around thirty-nine.

Colter surrendered but his partner kept fighting, killing one of their leaders. The Blackfeet in turn killed Potts and one of the warrior leaders asked Colter how fast he could run. He was stripped naked, given a thirty second start, and told to run for his life. With thorny bushes and sharp rocks tearing at his unprotected skin and bare feet, Colter did just that, heading for the Madison River, five miles (eight km) away, with the Blackfeet close behind him. After three miles (five km) he had outrun all but one warrior, who he tripped and killed with the warrior's own lance. Colter then hid in the icy river under a pile of driftwood until the Blackfeet gave up the search. When they were gone, he swam downriver and started running again.

"Colter's Hell," an area of fumaroles and hot springs on the Shoshone River near Cody, Wyoming.

HUGH GLASS, A TALE OF TRUE GRIT

TOUGH AS COLTER WAS, SOME

WERE EVEN TOUGHER. SUCH WAS HUGH GLASS. NO ONE KNOWS WHERE HE WAS BORN OR WHO HIS PARENTS WERE—SOME SAY HE MIGHT HAVE BEEN OF IRISH DESCENT—NOR ANYTHING ABOUT HIS early life, other than that he might have been a pirate in the Gulf of Mexico with Jean Lafitte (and then again, maybe not). What is known for sure is that he was reckless and insubordinate, rugged, and self-reliant, and that in 1823 he joined an expedition up the Missouri River led by fur trader William H. Ashley.

WOUNDED IN a battle with Arikara Native Americans—"Rees," as they were known—he recovered in time to join a party sent to relieve a group of hunters at Fort Henry, at the mouth of the Yellowstone River. Glass was attacked and mauled by a grizzly bear, so badly that it seemed impossible he could live. Ashley knew he and his men could not safely remain much longer in the land of the Arikara, who after past encounters were hostile to the settlers, and asked for two volunteers to stay with the dying man until the end. John Fitzgerald and young Jim Bridger stepped forward.

Attacked by a grizzly bear.

Crossing the Divide (*Alfred Jacob Miller, 1810–74*).

They stayed with Glass until he died, or until they thought he was dead, then took his rifle, his ammunition, and his other possessions, loaded them into their own packs, and left. But Hugh Glass was not dead. He regained consciousness to find himself totally alone in the wilderness. Fortunately for him there was water in a nearby spring and berries on the trees he could eat, and ten days later he was ready to begin what would become an epic journey. Racked by pain and fever, passing in and out of consciousness, he set out for the only place in that wilderness where he could get help, Fort Kiowa, a trading post on the Missouri River, some 200 miles (320 km) away.

According to legend, Glass got lucky and happened upon a buffalo calf that had just been brought down by wolves. He drove the wolves off by setting fire to the grass, and remained by the carcass, gorging on buffalo meat, until his wounds began to heal. Then he moved on, crawling maybe a mile a day, sometimes two or three as his strength grew. Living on roots, berries, carrion, whatever he could find on the land, he crawled, staggered, and limped an incredible 300 miles (480 km) down the Grand River toward the Missouri. There, they say, he was befriended by Sioux Native Americans, who took him the rest of the way to Fort Kiowa.

No one now knows all the facts, but that it happened is not in question. Astonishingly, the adventures of Hugh

Glass were anything but over. Once fully recovered, he determined to go back up the river and avenge himself upon Jim Bridger and John Fitzgerald, the two men who had abandoned him. He joined up with a small party going north to the Mandan villages; they were attacked by a large band of Rees and all the traders were killed except for Glass and Toussaint Charbonneau, the husband of Sacajawea.

Glass continued north to Fort Henry, only to find it had been abandoned; a scrawled note on the gate told him Ashley's new headquarters were in the Big Horn country of Montana. On he went until he reached his destination and there found Jim Bridger, who was understandably terrified by this apparent return from the dead. After hearing Jim's side of things, Glass forgave Jim because of his youth, but set out to find the faithless Fitzgerald, half a continent away.

Heading south, having one narrow escape after another (and again being reported dead when he was not), he eventually located Fitzgerald, who had enlisted in the U.S. Army, at Fort Atkinson near what is now Omaha, Nebraska. There, legend has it, "To the man he addressed himself as he did to the boy [Bridger]—'Go, false man and answer to your own conscience and to your God; I have suffered enough in all reason by your perfidy.'"

Repossessing his rifle from Fitzgerald, Glass rode off to the southwest, where he later traded around Santa Fe and trapped in Ute country. He was again dangerously wounded, this time by a Native American arrow; yet again he survived and returned to the Yellowstone River area. In the winter of 1832–33 his old enemies the Rees—and fate—caught up with him, killing and scalping Glass and two companions as they were crossing the frozen river. It was the end of a legend and, in a way, the beginning of the end of the era of the mountain men.

THE GREAT PATHFINDERS

Caravan: Trappers Crossing the River
(Alfred Jacob Miller, 1810–74).

JOSEPH R. WALKER, TRAILBLAZER

ONCE THE FUR TRADE BEGAN

TO DECLINE, THE MOUNTAIN MEN NEEDED A NEW ROLE. MAKING THE MOST OF THEIR INTIMATE KNOWLEDGE OF THE LAND, THEY BECAME SCOUTS AND PATHFINDERS FOR THE MILITARY EXPEDITIONS THAT were sent out with increasing frequency to map and quantify the new areas, or for the growing numbers of emigrant parties setting out for the western territories. Among the most notable of these was Joseph Reddeford Walker, a pathfinder who opened up huge new areas of the unexplored continent.

BORN IN TENNESSEE in 1798, Walker moved with his family to Missouri in 1819, and accompanied a party of hunters and trappers to New Mexico a year or two later. After helping to chart and mark the Santa Fe trail, he served briefly as the sheriff of Independence, Missouri, a town he is said to have named. In February 1831, he set out on a trading expedition in Cherokee country, where he met Captain Benjamin Bonneville, an army officer who was planning a fur-trading

Joseph R. Walker, mountain man and experienced scout.

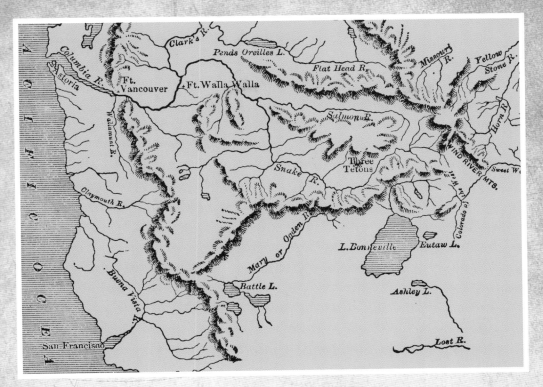

operation in the Rockies financed by wealthy New York businessmen.

Bonneville put Walker in charge of an expedition to California which—although Bonneville's reasons for mounting it are not known—was remarkably successful. They gained the Humboldt River by a route that would later be followed by countless emigrant trains, survived an attack by Paiute Native Americans, crossed the Sierra Nevada, and discovered

Benjamin Bonneville's Map of the American West, from The Adventures of Captain Bonneville *(1837).*

Paiute Native American encampment at Ten Mile River, Yosemite Valley.

This map of the United States in 1855 shows a number of important emigrant routes, including the Santa Fe Trail, the Oregon Trail, and Frémont's Route.

the Yosemite Valley and the giant sequoia trees there. After wintering in San Juan Bautista, the expedition returned via the San Joaquin Valley, crossing the Sierra at Walker's Pass and picking up their former trail, which they followed back, bringing with them much new geographical information about the country they had seen.

For fifty years, from the rise of the mountain men to the era of the cowboy, Joe Walker roamed the West, from the Mississippi to Mexico, and from prairie to desert to ocean, often turning up at crucial moments to extricate less experienced explorers from their difficulties. Following the demise

Glacier Point and South Dome, Yosemite Valley, California.

of the big fur-trading operations, he made horse-trading trips to California, trapped furs out of Fort Bridger, and accompanied explorer John Charles Frémont on two of his expeditions. Walker later ranched in California, guided troops in the 1859 campaign against the Mojave Native Americans, and in 1861 organized the group that would open up central Arizona. Throughout his life his "chief delight was to explore unknown regions." When Walker died in 1872, it must have given him considerable satisfaction to know that it was largely over trails he had discovered that Americans flooded into the country and created, in 1850, the state of California.

GOLD RUSH

In 1862–63, Joseph Walker led an expedition of thirty-four men into the mountains of central Arizona in search of gold. In his earlier quest for beaver skins, Walker had skirted most of the territory and on one trip in the late 1830s, while searching for water, had discovered what appeared to be yellow pebbles in a stream. They struck gold along the Hassayampa River and Lynx Creek, and a sizeable settlement grew up in the area once word had got around about their find. The village of Walker, Arizona, is named after the legendary scout.

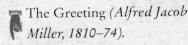 The Greeting (*Alfred Jacob Miller, 1810–74*).

"THE GREAT PATHFINDER"

JOHN CHARLES FRÉMONT WAS

BORN IN SAVANNAH, GEORGIA, IN 1813. EXPELLED FROM COLLEGE FOR "INCORRIGIBLE NEGLIGENCE," HE SECURED A COMMISSION IN THE U.S. ARMY'S TOPOGRAPHICAL CORPS AND JOINED JOSEPH Nicollet's 1838 expedition to explore Minnesota and Dakota. In 1841 he married Jessie, daughter of Senator Thomas Hart Benton; she became his most fervent supporter and Benton his most powerful ally. Through their influence Frémont was appointed to lead a reconnaissance to South Pass, in Wyoming, with Kit Carson as guide.

JOHN FRÉMONT'S

second expedition took place in 1842. Guided again by Carson along with Thomas Fitzpatrick, they traversed Wyoming and Idaho to Oregon and Fort Vancouver, then headed south into California's San Joaquin Valley before returning to St. Louis. It was this journey that made Frémont, "The Great Pathfinder," famous.

Kit Carson, intrepid frontiersman, who left home at age sixteen and became a mountain man and trapper.

Frémont's third expedition crossed the Sierra Nevada into California, at the time governed by Mexico. He was expelled by the Mexican authorities (relations between the United States and Mexico over the U.S. annexation of Texas were hostile) and retreated north. Receiving a secret message from President Polk, Frémont reentered California and supported the so-called Bear Flag Revolt. When war with Mexico was declared, Frémont's "California Battalion" took part in the capture of Los Angeles. Shortly after the end of hostilities, Frémont became involved in a conflict of authority and General Stephen Kearny had him arrested and court martialled for disobedience and mutiny. Found guilty, Frémont bitterly resigned his commission.

John Charles Frémont.

BEAR FLAG REVOLT

Frémont arrived in the Mexican-controlled territory of California, officially on a mapping expedition, but he actively encouraged the Anglo-American settlers to rebel against the Mexican authorities and declare California an independent republic. On June 14, 1846, a party of heavily armed men captured the Mexican garrison of Sonoma and arrested General Vallejo, former commandante of the territory. Led by William B. Ide, the rebels raised a crude homemade flag depicting a grizzly bear (representing strength and courage) and a star similar to the star on the Texas flag (California's ally against Mexico), emblazoned with the words "California Republic."

However, the republic was to prove short-lived. Frémont soon took command in the name of the United States, and on July 9, the Bear Flag was replaced by the Stars and Stripes. Just three weeks after it had been proclaimed, the California Republic quietly faded away, but the bear flag was to prove far more enduring and was officially adopted by the state of California in 1911.

In the winter of 1848, Frémont led a fourth, privately equipped expedition to find a route for a railroad across the Rockies. Trapped by snow, eleven of his men perished, including mountain man "Old Bill" Williams, who Frémont blamed for misdirecting them.

Elected one of California's first senators in 1850–51, in 1853 Frémont mounted his fifth expedition to California. In 1856 he won a presidential nomination, but lost to James Buchanan. When the Civil War began, Frémont resumed his

Presidential campaign poster— Frémont planting the American flag on the Rocky Mountains (1856).

army career, but his record was poor, mainly due to his own lack of judgment. Following the war he lost the remains of his personal fortune in bad investments. Appointed governor of Arizona in 1878, after five years he returned to California. In 1890 the U.S. Congress awarded him a pension, but he died shortly afterward, his successes as "The Great Pathfinder" earlier largely forgotten.

PUSHING WESTWARD

*Emigrants moved westward in covered wagons,
often known as "Prairie Schooners."*

BLAZING THE OREGON TRAIL

THE STREAM OF EMIGRANTS

HEADING WEST INTO THE NEW TERRITORIES BEGAN TO GROW AS THE U.S. ARMY LAID OUT ROADS AND BUILT STRATEGICALLY SITED FORTS TO PROTECT THEM. THE RANKS OF THE SETTLERS WERE SWOLLEN BY thousands of Europeans fleeing revolution and upheaval, seeking new hope and a new future in America. Once the main trails were well and truly established, the stream became an unstoppable torrent of emigration that would continue unabated for another forty years.

BY THE LATE 1820s, riverboats were pushing ever farther up the navigable rivers and wagons were regularly plying the trail originally blazed by William Becknell from Independence, Missouri, to Santa Fé in New Mexico, where commerce had boomed following the discovery of gold near Taos. In 1832 Nathaniel Wyeth led the first wagon train across the plains to the Pacific Northwest, following the route charted by Jedediah Smith that became known as "The Oregon Trail."

This historic trail, carved out by trappers, fur traders, and pathfinders,

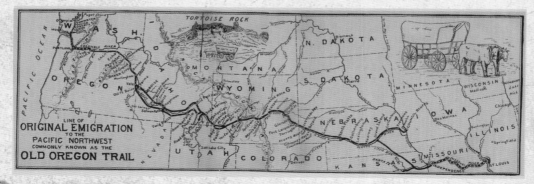

☞ *A wagon train is led past rock formations in a reenactment of the Oregon Trail.*

ran east–west from the Missouri River to the valleys of Oregon. Some 2,000 miles (3,200 km) long, at first it was only passable on foot or by horseback, but eventually a wagon trail was laid along the whole route. From around 1836, it is thought over 400,000 settlers made their way along the trail, but the first year of significant migration was 1843 and it continued well into the 1860s. The settlers were joined by missionaries, traders, and ranchers. Many Mormon emigrants also used the trail when their community moved to the Great Salt Lake region.

Covering an average of 15–20 miles (24–32 km) a day, the journey usually took four or five months. Most people left in spring as it was crucial to complete the extremely hazardous journey before the first snowfall.

Nathaniel Wyeth.

THE LONG TREK WEST

SETTLERS FROM EVERY STATE

ON THE MAP WERE ON THE MOVE, IN EVER-INCREASING NUMBERS, SO THAT BY THE 1840s EMIGRATION HAD BECOME A FACT OF LIFE. THEY PUSHED THE "FRONTIER" OUT TO TEXAS ACROSS PRESENT-DAY Kansas and Nebraska. The Oregon Trail and the Sante Fe Trail were the two main routes, with others branching off them, such as farther north to the Great Salt Lake in what is now Utah or south to destinations in the Mexican-controlled territory of California.

IN A VIVID word-picture, historian Francis Parkman described traveling upriver to Independence. In St. Louis, "the hotels were crowded, and the gunsmiths and saddlers were kept constantly at work in providing arms and equipment for the different parties of travelers." On that April day in 1846, the steamboat Radnor "was loaded until the water broke alternately over the guards. Her upper deck was covered with large wagons of a peculiar form, for the Santa Fe

☞ *Pilgrims on the plains, their possessions packed into wagons.*

trade, and her hold was crammed with goods for the same destination. There were also equipments and provisions of a party of Oregon emigrants, a band of mules and horses, piles of saddles and harness."

In the boat's cabin were, he wrote, "Santa Fe traders, gamblers, speculators, and adventurers of various descriptions," while the steerage area at the stern—where travelers who bought the cheapest tickets were crammed in—"was crowded with Oregon emigrants, 'mountain men,' negroes and a party of Kansas Indians, who had been on a visit to St. Louis." In Westport and Independence, the wagon trains kept saddlers and cobblers, blacksmiths and gunmakers, outfitters and map sellers busy; an outfitter in the small town of

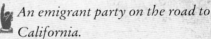 *An emigrant party on the road to California.*

Liberty, Missouri, declared he needed two thousand pounds of bacon a week to keep up with demand.

From the river the wagon trains moved out across the flat, baking, featureless plains. Their route took them along the Kansas River (to where Fort Kearney would be built in 1848 to protect the trail), then followed the Platte River to Fort Laramie and on to the headwaters of the Sweetwater River. Over South Pass in the Wind River Mountains they rumbled, and on to Fort Bridger, established in 1842, then along the trail pioneered by Wyeth and the mountain men to Fort Hall, along the Snake River to Fort Boise, and

THE OATMAN FAMILY

Many Native Americans were tolerant of the pioneer wagon trains that crossed their lands. Some traded and swapped buffalo robes and moccasins for knives, clothes, food, and other items. But violent altercations between the Native Americans and the pioneers did sometimes take place.

On such episode occurred in April 1851, when the Oatman family, consisting of father, mother, two sons, and four daughters were attacked by a band of Tonto Apaches as they crossed the Gila River. The two adults, two daughters, and one son were killed on the spot, the other son was left for dead. After looting the wagons, the Apaches took the two surviving girls, Olive and Mary Ann, with them, later selling them to some Mojave Native Americans. Lorenzo, the wounded son, was rescued and when he recovered from his wounds, began to search for his sisters. He found Olive five years later, by now tattooed on the face, as was tribal custom. Sadly, the younger girl, Mary Ann, had died of hardship and exposure.

overland to Fort Walla Walla at the confluence of the Snake and Columbia rivers. Finally, they would follow the Columbia in the footsteps of Lewis and Clark to Fort William, where the city of Portland stands today.

Emigrants to California followed the same route as far as Fort Hall, then turned southwest, bypassing the Great Salt Lake that Jim Bridger had once thought was the Pacific Ocean. They then followed the Humboldt River across what

A Native American chief, forbids the passage of a wagon train through his country.

Mormon pioneers coming off Big Mountain into Mountain Dell, Utah, July 1847.

would later become Nevada, then up through the Sierra Nevada and down the western slope to Sutter's Fort near Sacramento and, later, to San Francisco.

Whichever route the emigrants took, their journey was slow and fraught with danger. Many would-be settlers died as a result of accident or disease—there are no reliable statistics but some estimate that up to ten percent of all those who set out may have died en route. Every night the wagons would be formed into a protective square or circle, surrounding the animals inside. Conflict with Native Americans was in fact quite rare and many tribespeople

even helped the emigrants as they crossed tribal lands. However, in 1854 an incident near Fort Laramie had serious repercussions. A group of U.S. soldiers entered a Sioux encampment to arrest a man accused of killing one of the migrant's cows. A nervous soldier opened fire and in the fighting that ensued Chief Conquering Bear was mortally wounded and Lieutenant John Grattan and his entire command of twenty-nine men and an interpreter were killed. It was to become one of the first conflicts of the Sioux Wars.

Rivers could flood, wagons break down, and animals die. Asiatic cholera, dysentery, snakebites, an accidentally broken bone, or frostbite in the freezing mountain passes could all spell disaster and even death—and often did.

It was said that by 1850 there were four graves to the mile between St Joseph, Missouri, and Fort Laramie.

In the beginning, these primitive transcontinental highways were not so much marked as "known" by the guides and scouts—many of them onetime mountain men—that the emigrants hired to take them across country. But not all the guides were as experienced and knowledgeable as they made out, such as Lansford W. Hastings, an author-adventurer who had accompanied a wagon train to Oregon in 1842, and then moved to California.

In 1845 he touted a new, shorter route to California in his book *The Emigrants' Guide to Oregon and California* and set himself up as a guide at Fort Bridger to take emigrants along a route he modestly called the "Hastings cut-off," which would reduce their journey time considerably. In 1846 this unreliable "guide" led a wagon train organized in Springfield, Illinois. As a result, the Donner Party became one of the most tragic episodes in the history of the American West (see page 51).

Settlers setting up camp for the night on their arduous journey.

THE BATTLE OF THE ALAMO

The final assault on the beleaguered defenders of the Alamo, March 6, 1836.

FANNING THE FLAMES OF REBELLION

IN THE MID-1820s, EMIGRANTS FLOODED SOUTH FROM VIRGINIA, THE CAROLINAS, AND KENTUCKY INTO TEXAS, THEN PART OF COAHUILA, MEXICO. THE NEWCOMERS HAD LITTLE IN COMMON WITH THE RESIDENT MEXICAN POPULATION and their differences came to a head when the Mexicans passed new laws designed to discourage further immigration and stationed troops to enforce them. The Texians (as Texans were known at the time of the Texas Revolution of 1835–36) refused to accept Mexican authority and began moving toward rebellion and, ultimately, independence. The fire of revolt was lit when the president of Mexico, General Antonio López de Santa Anna Pérez de Lebrón, passed laws ordering the Texians to surrender their firearms to the military.

WHEN A COMPANY of soldiers commanded by Captain Mario Castañeda was sent to the small town of Gonzales to enforce this policy and reclaim an old cannon that had been loaned to the town by the military, they were greeted by the muzzle of that same cannon, fully primed, beneath a banner inviting them to: "Come and get it!"

In response, Santa Anna immediately sent an army commanded by his brother-in-law General Martin Perfecto de Cos to "finish off" the Texian troublemakers. The Texians responded by forming a volunteer army. Led by "Old Indian Fighter" Colonel Edward Burleson, the untrained army laid siege to the town of San Antonio de Béxar, where the troops of Cos were stationed. The Alamo—as the Spanish mission was known—stood nearby.

The weather was bad, with continuous rain, and there wasn't enough food. The volunteers began to talk about going

General Antonio López de *Santa Anna, president of Mexico.*

home—there seemed no likelihood of any real fighting and they could soon return if it did break out. However, the provisional government offered the volunteers $20 per month to stay on and so they remained.

Two men escaped from the town and reported that the Mexican troops were starving, low on ammunition, and in poor spirits. It was at this point that veteran soldier Ben Milam rallied the Texians. "Who will come with Old Ben Milam into San Antone?" he roared. They attacked at dawn on December 5, 1835, driving the Mexicans out of the town—where Milam was killed by a sniper—and into the Alamo, where a week later they surrendered.

The chapel of the Alamo, San Antonio de Béxar, Texas.

THE SIEGE BEGINS

THE MISSION SAN ANTONIO

DE VALERO—THE ALAMO—WAS ESTABLISHED IN 1718. IT MAY HAVE BEEN NAMED FOR THE GROVE OF COTTONWOOD TREES IN WHICH IT STOOD (*ÁLAMO* IS SPANISH FOR "COTTONWOOD"), OR BECAUSE it was used as a barracks by Mexican troops from Álamo de Parras during the Mexican War for Independence. The four-acre mission included adobe barracks, a convent, and the chapel, surrounded by walls. It was abandoned in 1793, although the roof had fallen in, the walls were still firm and stout, and the convent buildings were in fair repair.

FOLLOWING THE SIEGE of San Antonio, the Alamo became the headquarters of the Texians, or at least of those who remained in the town; on December 20, 1835, some two hundred of their fellows decided to follow commander Colonel Frank W. Johnson on a freebooting expedition into Mexico, taking most of the existing supplies, clothing, and money with them. Johnson handed the command to Colonel James C. Neill who, knowing he

did not have enough men to hold his position against the Mexican army that was being formed, wrote to the Texas governor asking for reinforcements or permission to retreat.

Aware that San Antonio would be Santa Anna's first objective, Governor

🖎 *The mission of San Antonio de Valero.*

44

The Alamo.

Henry Smith concluded that if Santa Anna could be forced to leave the town in Texian hands, such a defeat might well destroy his power and the confidence of his army. And there was another factor: the Texian army was still anything but strong. General Samuel Houston needed time to recruit enough men to face Santa Anna and defeat him. Consequently, the Alamo must not be abandoned.

Instead, in January, 1836, the young, ambitious Colonel William Barret Travis was ordered to take command of the Alamo. Travis hesitated: he was, he wrote to the governor "unwilling to risk my reputation (which is ever dear to a soldier), by going into the enemy's country with such little means, with so few men, and them so badly equipped."

Nevertheless, he went, taking thirty recruits with him. Travis was nearly thirty-four years of age, and already had a reputation as a firebrand. When he arrived at the Alamo, he found himself in the difficult position of having to share his responsibilities with Colonel James Bowie, who had taken command of the volunteers and was senior in age and service.

Soldier of fortune Jim Bowie, born in Kentucky in 1795, had come to Texas in search of the lost San Saba mine, and in 1828 married Ursula, the daughter of Juan Martin de Veramendi. In 1833, however, his wife and children died in a cholera epidemic and he left Texas, returning a year later to join the Texians in their fight for independence, even though he was a staunch friend of the Mexicans. Somewhere along the line, Bowie made or acquired the large knife that together with his exploits would make his name legendary.

On February 23, the advance guard of Santa Anna's five-thousand-strong army reached San Antonio and drove the Texians from the town to the shelter of the mission. Shortly after this, David "Davy" Crockett arrived

45

🔊 *Davy Crockett.*

for Texas, the other for Coahuila) instead of the Mexican eagle and serpent. Santa Anna replied by hoisting a blood-red flag with a black skull and crossbones, a signal that "no quarter" would be given—no surrender would be accepted, no mercy given—and began bombarding the beleaguered mission before retiring to formulate his plans for the attack on the Alamo.

The next day, Colonel Travis wrote this now famous letter:

at the Alamo with nineteen men, the "Tennessee Mounted Volunteers." Crockett's name was already legendary. Born in Tennessee in 1786, his colorful career had already included marriage to Polly Finley (a descendant of Macbeth, king of Scotland), election to the Territorial Legislature in 1821, and later also to Congress. He was close to fifty years of age at this time.

On February 23, the Mexican army positioned itself around the walls of the mission, and Santa Anna demanded the surrender of the garrison. Travis answered with a cannon shot, and the hoisting of the new flag, a white, red, and green banner with two stars (one

TO THE PEOPLE OF TEXAS AND ALL AMERICANS IN THE WORLD:

Fellow citizens and compatriots—I am besieged by a thousand or more Mexicans under Santa Anna—I have sustained a continual bombardment and cannonade for twenty-four hours and have not lost a man—the enemy has demanded surrender at discretion, otherwise the garrison is to be put to the sword if the fort is taken—I have answered the demands with a cannon shot, and our flag still waves proudly from the walls—I shall never surrender or retreat. Then, I call upon you in the name of liberty, of patriotism, and everything dear to the American character, to come to our aid with all dispatch—the enemy is receiving reinforcements daily, and will no doubt increase to three or four thousand in four or five days. If this call is neglected, I am determined to sustain myself as long as possible, and die like a soldier who never forgets what is due his own honor and that of his country—victory or death.

William Barret Travis

Travis sent his old school friend James Butler Bonham to enlist the aid of Colonel James W. Fannin, stationed at Goliad. Fannin set off, but after a series of accidents and unable to get his artillery across the swollen rivers, he reluctantly turned back. When Bonham prepared to return to the Alamo, Fannin tried to stop him. "I will report to Travis or die in the attempt," Bonham said, and set out immediately.

Bonham got back on the afternoon of March 3, and his news was passed to the men—reinforcements were on the way (in fact, they never arrived). The news in the Mexican camp was of the arrival of three more battalions, reinforcing Santa Anna's army by nearly a thousand men. Tradition—and it may be no more than that—has it that at this point, Travis drew a line in the sand with his sword, and invited all those who would stay with him to fight to step across to his side. Every man bar one stepped across. Confined to bed with an unidentifiable illness, Jim Bowie asked to be lifted over the line in his cot.

Travis wrote to a friend in Washington County asking him to take care of his son: "If the country should be saved, I may make him a splendid fortune, but if the country should be lost and I should perish, he would have nothing but the proud recollection that he is the son of a man who died for his country. I shall continue to hold the Alamo until I get relief from my countrymen or I perish in its defense…." He also wrote to the newly assembled Convention at Washington-on-the-Brazos to say he felt confident: "that the determined valor and desperate courage heretofore shown by my men will not fail them in the last struggle; and although they may be sacrificed to the vengeance of a Gothic enemy, the victory will cost him so dear, that it will be worse for him than a defeat. For liberty and honor, God and Texas, victory or death!"

Melodramatic? Perhaps—but remember those words were written as shells burst against the walls of the Alamo, and rain poured down on the men huddled below, watching the glowing lights of a thousand campfires.

Col. William Barret Travis.

THE FINAL BATTLE

BY THE 11TH DAY OF THE SIEGE,

ON MARCH 4, THE GARRISON WAS SURROUNDED AND ITS WATER SUPPLY CUT OFF. CANNONBALLS BATTERED THE MISSION AND A CONTINUOUS FUSILLADE FROM THE MEXICAN RIFLEMEN WAS maintained against the Texians. Santa Anna and his generals determined their final assault. When General Juan Almonte, Santa Anna's aide, remarked that he feared the attack would cost them dear, Santa Anna snapped it was of "no importance what the cost was, it must be done."

AT DAWN on March 6, the band struck up the assassin's song and bugle call, "El Degüello" (from the Spanish *degollar*, to cut someone's throat), confirmation of Santa Anna's instruction that no quarter was to be given. The rocket battery fired to signal the start of the assault and the peaceful Sunday morning was suddenly shattered as the Texians rushed to their posts on the walls and the Mexican troops under General Manuel Fernández Castrillón moved toward them.

The Toluca Battalion, heading the attack, fell back hastily as the deadly fire of the Texian riflemen devastated their ranks.

General Cos came up, and split half his force into four columns. He was to make simultaneous attacks on the east and west sides, while the main attack would come from forces massed on the plain to the north.

Realizing that the east and west attacks were intended to distract their forces, the Texians rushed to the north wall to repel the main attack, whereupon Santa Anna threw reinforcements against the east wall, and it was there that cannon fire made the first breakthrough. Bonham and Travis, both manning artillery, were killed in this attack, the latter by a shot through the forehead.

Jim Bowie.

Battle of the Alamo (*Percy Moran, 1862–1935*).

Santa Anna now ordered a renewed assault on the north walls and as the Mexican troops poured in, the battle became a series of isolated hand-to-hand encounters. Some sixty Texians escaped the Alamo buildings, but heading east on the Gonzales road were cut down by the Mexican cavalry. Jim Bowie was bayoneted to death on his sickbed, fighting to the last. Robert Evans, detailed to blow up the powder magazine, was killed on the threshold of the chapel. Davy Crockett and a band of men had retreated to the chapel and Crockett fell near it, surrounded by dead Mexicans.

Historians still argue over a suggestion that Crockett did not die fighting, but that he was one of five (or seven) men who offered to surrender on condition that their lives be spared. However, Santa Anna was said to have spurned them and they were cut to pieces with cavalry sabres.

When the ceasefire bugles finally sounded an hour and a half after the battle had begun, the dead and wounded were littered everywhere across the scene. At the time Mexican losses were variously estimated at between one and three thousand men, although it is more likely that the total was in the region of possibly sixty or seventy killed and perhaps three hundred wounded. Santa

Susanna Dickinson, one of only three American survivors of the battle.

Anna refused to bury the American dead and gave orders that they be put into a pile and burned.

Don José Francisco Ruiz, *alcalde* (mayor) of San Antonio, later wrote: "about three o'clock in the afternoon we laid wood and dry branches upon which the pile of dead bodies was placed, more wood was piled on them, and another pile of bodies was brought and in this manner they were all arranged in layers. Kindling wood was distributed throughout the pile and about five o'clock … it was lighted."

The funeral pyre was still burning as the Mexicans moved out from the Alamo, taking with them the wife of the gunnery officer, Susanna Dickinson, her daughter Angelina, and Travis's servant Joe, the only Americans to survive the carnage (although some ten or more Mexicans also came out alive). Eventually under a light breeze the ashes of the nearly two hundred brave men who died there—not just Americans, but English, Scots, Irish,

German, and Danish too— were blown gently across the yard, which today many Americans regard as hallowed ground.

By holding Santa Anna's army at bay and inflicting such grave casualties, the men who died at the Alamo, who never even knew that Texas had declared its independence from Mexico on March 2, while the battle was still raging, gave the wavering Texians a breathing space and a cause. Bold, shrewd General Sam Houston hit the right note when he addressed his army just forty-six days later, on the eve of what would be the decisive conflict of the Texas Revolution, the Battle of San Jacinto. "Victory is certain!" he told them. "Trust in God and fear not! And remember the Alamo! Remember the Alamo!"

The next day the Texians routed the Mexican army and captured Santa Anna himself, shattering Mexico's hold upon the land. Today's Texians still "remember the Alamo" and the men who died there. And they will tell you proudly that those men were not defeated at all: they were only killed.

THE

DONNER PARTY

Summit of the Sierras, Nevada
(*Thomas Moran, 1837–1926*).

THE JOURNEY BEGINS

OF ALL THOSE WHO BRAVED

THE MANY HARDSHIPS OF THE WESTWARD TREK, NONE SUFFERED MORE THAN THE DONNER PARTY BOUND FOR CALIFORNIA, A GROUP OF EIGHTY-SEVEN MEN, WOMEN, AND CHILDREN, ORGANIZED AND led by two wealthy brothers, Jacob and George Donner, who loaded up their wagons in the summer of 1846.

ON MAY 11, 1846, George Donner's wife Tamsen sent her sister a letter of farewell from the bustling town of Independence:

> I can give you no idea of the hurry of the place at this time. It is supposed there will be 7000 waggons [sic] start from this place…
>
> We go to California, to the bay of Francisco. It is a four month trip. We have three waggons furnished with food and clothing and drawn by three yoke of oxen each… I am willing to go and have no doubt it will be an advantage to our children and to us.

Although Tamsen Donner was misinformed about the number of wagons leaving Independence that year (the figure was nearer 700 than 7,000), her excitement and anticipation are clear. On May 12, the Donner Party set off on their journey. The route they would follow was shaped—roughly speaking—like a rainbow, beginning in Missouri and ending in California, with the top of the arc at South Pass in Wyoming, 8,000 ft (2,439 m) high. On its western side the trail divided, the right fork leading to Oregon, the left heading to California.

The Donners had read Lansford W. Hastings's book *The Emigrants' Guide to Oregon and California* and contacted him to conduct them from

Fort Bridger, "thence bearing west southwest, to the Salt Lake; and thence continuing down to the Bay of St Francisco." When they reached the Fort on August 3, 1846, however, they learned that Hastings had already gone, leading another wagon train, but he had left word that he would mark the trail for them. They set out at once, following Hastings's trail.

Lansford W. Hastings.

At the Red Fork crossing of Weber River, they found a note left by Hastings jammed into a stick telling them the route ahead was very bad and asking them to wait; he would return shortly to show them a better and shorter route he had discovered through the Wasatch Mountains. They would soon discover that this, like all Hastings's promises, was an empty one.

Eight days later he had still not appeared, so the Donners decided to send three men—Charlie Stanton, Bill McCutchen, and James Reed, one of the leaders of the party—to find him.

The Wasatch mountain range stretches approximately 160 miles (260 km) through central Utah, south from the Utah-Idaho border.

They caught up with Hastings but he flatly refused to leave the wagon train he was with; instead he took James Reed to the summit of Big Mountain and showed him—by pointing—the best way to get through the mountains. Stanton and McCutchen remained with the Hastings party to rest their horses and Reed returned to the wagon train alone. A conference was called and it was decided to try the route Hastings had recommended.

The route—there was no trail—proved to be virtually impassable, clogged with willow and alder, and strewn with huge boulders. After heartbreaking hardships,

Crossing the Great Salt Lake Desert *(John J. Young).*

the Donner Party finally found their way through the Wasatch Range and reached the valley south of the Great Salt Lake, having taken what would be eighteen critical days to get there.

It took them another six days and nights to cross the empty salt desert—a journey the Hastings "guidebook" had told them would take two. To speed up their progress, the emigrants decided that most of the furniture and other valuables they had brought from Illinois would have to be abandoned, along with four wagons and most of the livestock, which had stampeded for water when they were unyoked. The days were murderously hot and the nights freezing. And there was still no word from Hastings.

James Reed, a wealthy Irish immigrant, was traveling with his wife Margaret, five children, and his mother-in-law Sarah Keyes.

McCutchen and Stanton, now back with the train, were sent ahead to get help and food from Sutter's Fort, while the rest of the party—now down to fifteen wagons from the original twenty-three—struggled onward to the base of the Sierra Nevada, as geese on their way south honked ominously overhead.

By now the emigrants were exhausted, both physically and emotionally. Quarrels broke out, often over petty matters. In the course of trying to

prevent an argument between two of the men, James Reed stabbed one of them to death. Unpopular with many of the other settlers, Reed was banished as a result, leaving his wife and five children with the wagon train. He determined to try to get to California alone and bring help, and rode ahead of the party, crossing the Sierra just ahead of the early snows.

On October 19, "Little Charlie" Stanton, one of the two-man party who had left a month earlier to seek help in California, returned from Sutter's Fort with two Native American guides and five mules laden with much-needed supplies, giving the party new hope.

INTO THE MOUNTAINS

ON OCTOBER 23, THE PIONEERS

LEFT THE SALT DESERT BEHIND AND REACHED WATER. AHEAD LAY THE LONG CLIMB OVER THE MOUNTAINS. THE WAGONS WERE NOW STRUNG OUT IN SEVERAL GROUPS, EVERYONE ANXIOUS TO GET through the pass before it was closed by snow. To the desperate members of the Donner Party, it must have seemed that the worst of their troubles had passed, but by November 3 snow had already fallen.

PART OF THE group of twenty-one souls, twelve of them children, stopped in Alder Creek Valley; the larger group in the lead camped near a lake (now called Donner Lake) high in the mountains, ready for the final push through the pass and into the valley. That night, however, a month earlier than usual, the first storm of the winter struck, and it was a bad one.

William Eddy, who led the "Forlorn Hope" party.

The members of the party fashioned shelters from wagon canvas and huddled together to keep out the winter cold. It snowed for eight days, completely blocking the pass. Marooned a mile high in the Sierra Nevada, all they could do now was wait—and hope. By December 4, the snow was some eight feet deep. By the middle of the month, their situation was becoming ever more

desperate, and it was decided someone must go for help, or they would all die from hunger.

Seventeen of the strongest among them (ten men, five women, and two boys), who called themselves the "Forlorn Hope," set out on homemade snowshoes to try to reach Sutter's Fort, over a hundred miles away. Led by Will Eddy, they left on December 16 with six days' rations on what became a nightmare of privation and horror that eventually lasted thirty-two days.

On Christmas night they were caught in a violent storm. Totally lost and utterly exhausted, they had no food and no hope in such weather of finding

The summit of the Sierra Nevada, with Donner Lake in the distance.

any; two days later four of them were dead. The survivors had no choice; weeping, they cooked and ate flesh from the bodies. The remaining flesh was labeled so that no one would eat his kindred, and the band moved on. Two more men died, and eventually even the two Native Americans, who had steadfastly refused to touch human flesh, were shot and eaten. Finally, on January 10, 1847, in chilling rain the seven survivors happened upon a Native American village. A week later Will Eddy reached a settlement called Johnson's Ranch and help was sent for.

"FORLORN HOPE"

The members of the ill-fated "Forlorn Hope" rescue party who set out on foot in an attempt to cross the mountain pass. Two turned back before reaching the pass, eight died en route.

Antonio	age apprx. 23	died en route
Luis	age apprx. 19	died en route
Salvador	age apprx. 28	died en route
Charles Burger	age apprx. 30	turned back
Patrick Dolan	age apprx. 35	died en route
William Eddy	age apprx. 28	survived
Jay Fosdick	age apprx. 23	died en route
Sarah Fosdick	age 21	survived
Sarah Foster	age 19	survived
William Foster	age 30	survived
Franklin Graves	age 57	died en route
Mary Ann Graves	age 19	survived
Lemuel Murphy	age 12	died en route
William Murphy	age 10	turned back
Amanda McCutchen	age 23	survived
Harriet Pike	age 18	survived
Charles Stanton	age 30	died en route

Heavy storms blanketed the Sierra throughout January, so it was not until February that a seven-man relief party from Sutter's Fort led by Aquilla Glover reached the survivors—if the skeletal individuals now left could be called that. It was clear many were far too weak and ill to be brought out, so Glover and his men brought down only those who were strong enough to travel: three men, four women, and seventeen children. On the way down

Donner Pass in winter, some 7,088 ft (2,160 m) high.

Stumps of trees cut down by the Donner Party at Alder Creek. The height of the tree stumps indicates the depth of the snow.

they met McCutchen and James Reed, who were going up to the camps, taking desperately needed food and clothing.

The Glover party reached Sutter's Fort on March 4. In the meantime, Reed and McCutchen had got through to the lake camp, where they found evidence that the starving emigrants had also been reduced to cannibalism, as had those at the Alder Creek camp. Jacob Donner was dead and his brother George was dying. Although Reed begged her to come with him, Tamsen Donner would not leave her husband. The two men headed back down the mountain with fourteen children and three adults.

A fourth relief party led by William Fallon set out to bring down the remaining survivors on April 13. When they reached the lake camp they found distressing evidence of what the party had been forced to eat: twigs, bones, hides, wild animals, family pets, and, eventually, human remains. The lone survivor was German immigrant Lewis Keseberg, whom the rescuers suspected had cannibalized the remains of Tamsen Donner.

Fallon's party reached Sutter's Fort on April 26. Of the eighty-nine emigrants who had set out so optimistically from Fort Bridger, only forty-seven came through alive.

Lewis Keseberg, the sole survivor of the lake camp.

CONCLUSION

IT IS DIFFICULT TO IMAGINE A

TRAGEDY WORSE THAN THAT OF THE DONNER PARTY, BUT THERE WOULD BE MANY MORE LIKE IT AS THE WEST OPENED UP, AND DURING those early years it must have seemed as though it was doing so at an extraordinary pace.

IN 1845 THE United States acquired further huge areas of land when the Republic of Texas, which had defeated the Mexican army at San Jacinto six weeks after the fall of the Alamo, abandoned its original intention of remaining permanently independent and was annexed to become the twenty-eighth American state, just five days before James K. Polk took the presidential oath of office. The absorption of Texas, however, virtually guaranteed war with Mexico, which had never accepted the independence of its rebellious province.

The $100,000,000 war with Mexico was won when its capital was captured. This too seemed like Manifest Destiny: under the terms of Mexico's surrender—the Treaty of Guadalupe

James K. Polk, 11th president of the United States.

Hidalgo—the victorious United States appropriated the northern third of the republic, a vast tract of land comprising all of western Texas, Nevada, Utah, Arizona, and California, and parts of New Mexico, Colorado, and Wyoming.

The sum paid for this huge area—exactly the same amount that Thomas Jefferson had paid for Louisiana Territory— proved to be an even bigger bargain: just nine days before the treaty was signed, a man named James Marshall discovered gold in the American River at a settlement called Sutter's Mill, near what is now Coloma, California. A few months later when the news reached the east, the California Gold Rush began and the movement of Americans westward became an irresistible force.

GLOSSARY

Artillery Large guns (e.g. cannon) used to shoot over a long distance; the part of an army using these guns.

Commission An official document appointing the rank of officer, e.g. captain, colonel.

Emigrant/emigration Someone who leaves a country or region to live in another/the act of leaving a country or region.

Freebooting Stealing and plundering in a lawless manner.

Frontiersman/-woman Someone who lives on or near a frontier, a border separating two regions.

Fumarole An opening in volcanic rock through which hot gases escape.

Fusillade A series of shots fired at once or in quick succession.

Garrison A military base or fort; a group of troops stationed in the fort.

Headman The leader of a people or community.

Immigrant/immigration Someone who comes to a country to live there permanently/the act of coming to another country.

Manifest Destiny In the19th century, the belief that settlers of European ancestry were destined to settle across the American continents, and were justified in doing so.

Mission In the religious sense, the work of an organization (especially Christian) to spread its faith in the world; a building or buildings used by a Christian mission.

Missionary Someone sent to promote their religion (especially Christian) abroad.

Mormon A member of the Christian Church of Jesus Christ of Latter-day Saints founded by Joseph Smith in the United States in 1830.

Pony Express A rapid postal service operated by relays of horses and riders across the Western United States in 1860–61.

Powder magazine A room in which gunpowder is kept.

Rocket battery A grouping of rockets for military purposes.

Settler Someone who goes to live in a new place, usually uninhabited or with few people.

Topographical Relating to the physical features of an area of land (e.g. steepness of the land, rivers, lakes).

Trading post A place (e.g. store, fort, or settlement) far from other towns used as a center for buying and selling goods and services.

Trapper Someone who traps wild animals, usually for their fur.

FURTHER
INFORMATION

Bertozzi, Nick. *Lewis & Clark*. New York, NY: First Second, 2011.

Burrows, John. *Sterling Biographies: Lewis & Clark: Blazing a Trail West*. New York, NY: Sterling Publishers Inc, 2008.

Dulle, Ronald J. *Tracing the Santa Fe Trail: Today's Views, Yesterday's Voices*. Sevierville, TN: Mountain Press Publishing Company, 2010.

Hill, Rick & Frazier, Teri. *Indian Nations of North America*. Des Moines, IA: National Geographic, 2010.

Klausmeyer, David. *Oregon Trail Stories: True Accounts of Life in a Covered Wagon*. Guilford, CT: TwoDot, 2003.

Meeker, Ezra; Drigss, Howard R. *Ox-Team Days on the Oregon Trail*. Carlisle, MA: Applewood Books, 2001.

Moeller, Bill & Jan. *The Oregon Trail: A Photographic Journey*. Missoula, Montana: Mountain Press Publishing Company, 2001.

Murdoch, David. S *DK Eyewitness Books: North American Indian*. New York, NY: DK Children, 2005.

Rarick Ethan. *Desperate Passage: The Donner Party's Perilous Journey*. New York, NY: Oxford University Press, 2009.

Souza, Dorothy M. *John C. Fremont (Watts Library) Paperback*. New York, NY: Children's Press, 2004

Wallis, Michael. *David Crockett: The Lion of the West*. New York, NY: W. W. Norton & Company, 2012.

Web sites

The official website for The Alamo Shrine in San Antonio, Texas: www.thealamo.org

Lewis and Clark: further research and information:
http://lewisclark.net/
http://lewis-clark.org/
http://lewisandclarkjournals.unl.edu/
www.nationalgeographic.com/lewisandclark/

The Donner Party:
http://www.legendsofamerica.com/ca-donnerparty.html

The American West:
http://www.spartacus.schoolnet.co.uk/USAamericanwest.htm

Sutter's Fort State Historic Park: www.suttersfort.org

INDEX

Alamo, The 42–50, 60
Almonte, Juan 48
Arikara people 22, 24
Ashley, William Henry
    17, 22
Astor, John Jacob 16

Bear Flag Revolt 31
Becknell, William 34
Beckwourth, Jim 20
Benton, Jessie 30
Benton, Thomas Hart 30
Berthoud, Edward Louis 19
Billy the Kid (William H.
    Bonney) 19
Blackfoot people 13, 18, 19,
    20–21
Bonham, James Butler 47,
    48
Bonneville, Benjamin 26–27
Boone, Daniel 21
Bowie, James 45, 47, 48, 49
Bowie, Ursula 45
Bridger, Jim 17, 18–19, 22,
    24, 38
Buchanan, James 32
Burleson, Edward 42

California 8, 29, 30, 31–32,
    36
Carson, Kit 19, 30
Castañeda, Mario 42
Charbonneau, Jean Baptiste
    11, 14
Charbonneau, Lizette 14
Charbonneau, Toussaint 11,
    14, 24
Chouteau, Pierre 16
Clark, George Rogers 9

Clark, William 8–14
Colter, John 20–21
Columbia River 11, 12, 13,
    38
Conquering Bear 39
Cos, Martin Perfecto 42
Crockett, David "Davy"
    45–46, 49
Crockett, Mary "Polly"
    Finley 46
Crow people 20
Cruzatte, Pierre 13

Dickinson, Angelina 50
Dickinson, Susanna 50
Donner Party 40, 51–60
Donner, George 52, 59
Donner, Jacob 52, 59
Donner, Tamsen 52, 59

Eddy, William 56, 57
Evans, Robert 49

Fallon, William 59
Fannin, James Walker 47
Fernández Castrillón,
    Manuel 48
Fink, Mike 17
Fitzgerald, John 22, 24
Fitzpatrick, Thomas 17, 18
Flathead tribe 19
Floyd, Charles 9
Fort Bridger, Wyoming 19,
    29, 37, 40, 53
Frémont, John Charles 29,
    30–32, 32

Garrett, Pat 19
Glass, Hugh 17, 18, 22–24

Glover, Aquilla 58
Grattan, John 39
Great Salt Lake, Utah 18,
    35, 38

Hastings, Lansford Warren
    40, 52
Henry, Andrew 17
Houston, Samuel 45, 50
Humboldt River 27, 38

Ide, William Brown 31
Independence, Missouri
    26, 52

Jefferson, Thomas 8, 9, 10,
    11, 14, 60
Johnson, Francis White
    "Frank" 44
Johnson, John "Liver-
    Eating" 20
Johnston, Albert Sidney 19

Kearny, Stephen 31
Keseberg, Lewis 59
Keyes, Sarah 55

Lafitte, Jean 22
Lewis, Meriwether 8–14
Lisa, Manuel 16
Louisiana Territory 8, 14, 60

Mandan people 8–9, 14, 24
Marshall, James 60
McCutchen, Bill 53, 54, 59
Meek, Joe 19
Milam, Ben 43
Miller, Alfred Jacob 15, 20,
    23, 29

Missouri River 9, 11, 17, 12, 13, 22, 23, 35
Mojave people 29
Mormons 19, 35, 39

Napoleon I, Emperor of the French 8
Neill, James Clinton 44
Nez Perce people 13
Nicollet, Joseph 30

Oatman family 38
Oregon Trail 19, 28, 34–35, 36

Paiute people 27
Parkman, Francis 36
Polk, James Knox 31, 60
Potts, John 20–21
Powder River Expedition 19

Raynolds, William Franklin 19
Reed, James 53, 54, 55, 59

Reed, Margaret 55
Remington, Frederic 17
Rocky Mountains 11, 12, 13, 32
Ruiz, José Francisco 50

Sacajawea 10, 11, 14
Santa Anna Pérez de Lebrón, Antonio López de 42, 45, 46, 48, 49–50
Santa Fe Trail 26, 28, 36
Shoshone people 13
Sierra Nevada 27–28, 31, 39, 51, 55, 56
Sioux people 23, 39
Smith, Henry 45
Smith, Jedediah 17, 34
Stanton, Charlie 53, 54
Sublette, Milton 18
Sublette, William 17

Texas Revolution 42–50, 60
Tonto Apache people 38
Travis, William Barret 45, 46, 47, 48

Vallejo, Mariano Guadalupe 31
Vasquez, Louis 19
Veramendi, Juan Martin 45

Walker, Joseph Reddeford 26–29, 26
Wasatch Mountains 53–54
Williams, William S. "Old Bill" 20, 32
Wyeth, Nathaniel 34, 35, 37

Yellowstone Expedition 19
Yellowstone Park 18, 20
Yellowstone River 11, 13, 22, 24

Picture credits

Denver Public Library: 18
Geographicus Rare Antique Maps: 28
Gerblach Barklow Co., Joliet, Ill.: 49
Library of Congress: 8, 9, 10, 12, 13, 14, 17, 19, 24, 28 (btm), 30, 33, 36, 37, 38, 39, 40, 43 (btm), 45, 46, 49, 51, 57, 59, (top), 60
New York Public Library: 27
Shutterstock: 11, 53 (btm), 58
Smithsonian American Art Museum: 6
Texas State Library & Archives Commission: 50
University of Texas Libraries: 34
U.S. National Archives and Records Administration: 35 (top), 54
Walters Art Museum: 15, 23, 25, 29
All other media files are in the public domain in the United States. This applies to U.S. works where the copyright has expired, often because its first publication occurred prior to January 1, 1923. See http://copyright.cornell.edu/resources/publicdomain.cfm for further explanation.